Social Selling In The Digital Era

Using Social Media To Drive Sales And Grow Your Business

Isaac Finch

Table of Contents:

Introduction

It's great to have you here at **"Social Selling in the Digital Era: Using Social Media to Drive Sales and Grow Your Business."** The way we conduct business and interact with clients has dramatically changed in today's quick-paced, technologically advanced environment. The notion of selling has completely changed with the emergence of social media platforms, providing companies with previously unheard-of opportunities to engage with their target market and increase sales.

In this book, we will cover the methods, tactics, and insights required to successfully use social media platforms for generating leads and expanding your business. We will also dig into the dynamic world of social selling. No matter if you're an established salesperson, a small business owner, or an entrepreneur trying to increase your sales channels, this book will provide you with practical advice and tried-and-true methods for navigating the online world.

The internet world has completely changed how customers connect and make judgments about what to buy. Social networking sites like **Facebook, Instagram, LinkedIn, and Twitter** have ingrained themselves into our everyday lives and provide businesses with unmatched access to enormous client bases. Businesses can use social media to generate interesting content, forge connections, and eventually increase sales if they take the correct strategy.

We will lead you through the essential concepts of social selling in this book and provide you with the resources to create a strong social media strategy. We'll examine the essential components of a successful social media strategy, such as content production, audience targeting, engagement strategies, and performance evaluation. You'll discover how to use different social media channels to broaden your audience, build your brand, and boost conversions.

We will also explore the craft of using social media to create lasting connections. In the digital age, building connections and cultivating trust are key to effective selling. We will walk you through the steps of creating a real online presence, interacting with potential clients, and turning those contacts into brand-loyal promoters.

You'll find case studies and real-world examples from firms that have successfully used social selling strategies to generate exceptional sales growth in each chapter.

These real-world illustrations will show how companies of all sizes and sectors may apply social selling tactics and modify them to suit their own objectives and target markets.

The goal of **"Social Selling in the Digital Era"** is to provide you with the information and abilities needed to succeed in the cutthroat marketplace of today. You will be well-positioned to harness the power of social media and use it as a dynamic tool to boost sales, improve customer connections, and expand your business if you follow the guidelines and tactics presented in this book.

This book will be your reliable companion on this life-changing adventure, whether you're just starting in social selling or trying to improve your current strategy.

It's time to fully embrace the digital world and utilize social media to boost sales and the expansion of your company.

Understanding Social Selling

In social selling, ties are strengthened and new sales discussions are initiated. Salespeople may locate, interact with, and connect with potential consumers via social media platforms. These contacts can then lead to sales dialogues. In general, social selling aims to develop connections with prospects through real, face-to-face interactions that take place in online forums. Your sales representative has earned the right to request a meeting or phone contact to begin a sales conversation if they have built a rapport with a warm prospect that is based on trust.

The idea that social selling is just online marketing has persisted for a long time. Finding your target customers on social media networks and then pitching them a mass-market message about how your solutions may help them in the hopes that five out of a hundred will reply favourably is NOT social selling. This strategy doesn't work. The brand value of this strategy is compromised.

Define social selling:

Building your sales team's network, personalizing interactions, providing value, and including a pertinent call-to-action are all key components of social selling. These strategies eventually result in sales dialogues with target account decision-makers. As a result, we want to encourage you to encourage your sellers to establish their social selling cadence based on a "Ready, Aim, Fire" strategy rather than the (sadly) prevalent "ready, fire, aim" method.

Your sellers must approach sales like marketers.

Building brand recognition and inbound traffic for lead generation is a marketer's creed. Through a steady stream of information, content, and value, they want to be "attractive" to their target audience. Social sellers must behave like a vendor while thinking like a marketer. However, a marketer's communications flow from the brand to the marketplace is one-to-many. Social sellers, on the other hand, aim to entice decision-makers through focused and intentional one-to-one messages and involvement. As opposed to marketers who direct traffic to a website, social sellers direct prospects to their LinkedIn profile, which functions similarly to a website.

LinkedIn profiles for sellers should be built with customer-centric language that speaks to the problems of their intended customers. Their profile should make it crystal clear who they assist and why the consumer can rely on them for support. It needs to swiftly increase credibility with the customer.

When a social seller adopts a marketer's mentality in this area, they may communicate customer-centric value messaging to decision-makers before even engaging in dialogue, which increases their "attractiveness" with them. The main goal of effective social sellers is to initiate sales discussions with decision-makers. The "C2C" technique, or Connections to Conversations, is what we refer to as.

The Evolution of Selling in the Digital Era

Digital marketing: What Is It?
Digital marketing refers to the use of any digital channels by a business or organization to advertise or promote goods and services to customers. Digital marketing makes use of various websites, mobile devices, social media, search engines, and comparable platforms.
How Effective Is Online Marketing?

As digitization progressed, it was noted that fewer people were buying in person in the marketplaces, and today an increasing number of individuals are doing so for themselves and their families. Because you want to reach the correct audience and that audience is online, there are several benefits to advertising your company online.

Digital Marketing's Advantages

In a shorter amount of time, you may reach a wider audience. The clientele of conventional marketing departments and agencies has seen significant attrition as a consequence of technological advancements. Digital marketers have made the greatest progress in the places where people now use tablets, phones, and computers.

Digital marketing's past

In the 1990s, the phrase "digital marketing" initially appeared. With the advent of the internet and the creation of the Web 1.0 platform, the digital era began. Users of the Web 1.0 platform could obtain the information they needed, but they were unable to distribute it online. Marketers all around the globe were still wary of the digital platform up to that point. Since the internet had not yet seen broad adoption, they were unsure whether their techniques would be successful.

After the first clickable banner went up in 1993, HotWired bought a number of them to use in their advertising. This signalled the start of the shift from traditional marketing to digital marketing. This slow transformation allowed new technologies to join the digital market in 1994. Yahoo was introduced in the same year.

Yahoo, sometimes referred to as "Jerry's Guide to the World Wide Web" in honour of its creator Jerry Yang, had close to 1 million hits in its first year. As a result, there have been significant changes in the digital marketing sector, with businesses tweaking their websites to improve search engine ranks. More search engines and tools, including HotBot, LookSmart, and Alexa, were introduced in 1996.

In 1998, Google started to exist. Yahoo introduced Yahoo online search, whereas Microsoft introduced the MSN search engine. After the internet bubble burst two years later, all of the smaller search engines were either left behind or eliminated, making room for the industry's titans. The field of digital marketing had its first significant upswing in 2006 when it was estimated that search engine traffic had increased to roughly 6.4 billion in only one month. Microsoft established Live Search to compete with Google and Yahoo, pushing MSN on the back burner to not fall behind.

When Web 2.0 arrived, individuals started participating more actively rather than just being passive consumers. individuals may communicate with companies and other individuals using Web 2.0. 'Super information highway' and other such terms started to be used to describe the internet. As a consequence, the amount of information flowing through various channels, including those used by digital marketers, multiplied, and by 2004, internet advertising and marketing in the US alone generated almost $2.9 billion.

Social networking websites soon started to appear. The first social networking website was MySpace, which was quickly followed by Facebook. Many businesses understood that the influx of brand-new websites was starting to provide more options for them to sell their goods and brands. It opened up new economic opportunities and heralded the start of a new era in the history of commerce.

With additional resources, they need fresh ideas for brand promotion and social networking platform exploitation. Another significant turning point in the development of digital marketing was the cookie. Advertisers have started to explore other methods to profit from the nascent technology. One of these methods included tracking regular internet users' use patterns and typical browsing behaviours to create promotions and marketing materials that catered to their preferences. The purpose of the first cookie was to track user preferences. Cookies are now programmed to provide advertisers with several methods to get actual user data. The usage of cookies has evolved.

Customers may now access digitally advertised goods at any time. According to data gathered by the Marketing Tech Blog for 2014, social media posting is the most popular online activity in the US. The typical American uses social media for 37 minutes every day. 97% of digital marketers use Twitter, 69% use Pinterest, and 59% use Instagram. Facebook is used by 99% of them. Facebook has been a source of consumers for 70% of B2C marketers. The likelihood that 67% of Twitter users will purchase from a company is much higher. Luxury brands are represented on Pinterest in 83.8% of cases. LinkedIn, Twitter, and Facebook are the top three social media platforms utilized by marketers.

The Timeline of Digital Marketing Evolution

The 90s

Early in the 1990s, Archie, the first search engine, made its appearance, kicking off the search age. Quickly after came SEO, or search engine optimization.

In 1994, the first clickable online banners were released. With 3.5 million members upon debut, the first recognizable social networking platform was founded in 1997. Many websites that are still in use today were discovered in the 1990s, including Google and Yahoo's online searches, both of which launched in 1998.

Generation Millennial

In the new century, a massive economic bubble emerged. However, many firms suffered damage as the bubble peaked and broke between 2000 and 2002. As the economy recovered from the boom, several new websites were founded in the 2000s, including the first versions of LinkedIn in 2002, Myspace and WordPress in 2003, and Facebook in 2004. Mobile text message marketing grew in popularity in the early 2000s.

The Age of Mobile

Increased marketing and sales were seen in the second part of the decade, with Amazon's e-commerce sales reaching $10 billion. With the advent of

Whatsapp, Instagram, and Snapchat to the online community during the next several years, mobile app culture grew.

The Present Today

A person spends 65% of their time using digital media on a mobile device. Currently, the $200 billion digital advertising market is dominated by Google Ad Words, which generates 96% of the company's income. The digital marketing revolution has been spearheaded by social networking, which has an estimated 3.1 billion internet users. Influencer marketing is a $1 billion sector that has been fueled by the growth of blogs and Instagram and is expected to continue. In the next years, it is anticipated that the fascinating field of digital marketing will expand and undergo several new advancements.

How Social Media Transformed Sales

Without a doubt, social media has changed how sales are conducted in today's corporate environment. It has completely changed how businesses connect with their clients, sell their goods, and eventually generate income. We will examine how social media has altered corporate sales processes and tactics in this in-depth investigation.

1. **Increased Reach and Visibility:** The combined active user bases of social networking sites like Facebook, Instagram, Twitter, and LinkedIn total billions. Businesses now have an unrivalled chance to connect with customers across the world because of this enormous user base. Geographical boundaries that were formerly a key impediment to sales efforts are

now being broken down by companies' ability to communicate with prospective clients from all over the globe.

2. **Targeted Advertising:** Social networking sites gather a lot of information about their users, such as demographics, interests, and online activity. Businesses may construct highly focused advertising campaigns thanks to this data. Advertisers may target a specific demographic based on characteristics like age, region, hobbies, and even past purchases using tools like Facebook Ads Manager. Reaching prospective clients who are interested in the product or service being given is much more likely now that the targeting is so precise.

3. **Engagement and Interaction:** Social media has facilitated a medium for two-way contact between companies and their

clients. Companies may now have real discussions with their audience rather than relying just on conventional one-sided advertising. Through this contact, customers may get individualized customer support, product suggestions, and quick resolutions to questions or problems. Social media connection building may increase brand loyalty and repeat business.

4. **User-Generated Materials and Reviews:** Social media platforms promote the creation and dissemination of material about goods and services. Purchase choices may be greatly influenced by user-generated information, customer evaluations, and testimonials. While unfavourable evaluations might spur changes and improved customer service, positive comments and suggestions from

pleased clients can be powerful testimonials.

5. **E-commerce Integration:** Several social networking sites have included e-commerce functions like "Shop Now" buttons and in-app buying. Customers can now instantly purchase products via social media thanks to this frictionless connection, which speeds up the purchasing process. As consumers fulfil their want to purchase without leaving the site, this is especially advantageous for impulsive purchases.

6. **Data analytics and insights:** Social media offers companies powerful analytics capabilities to monitor the success of their sales and marketing initiatives. Businesses may monitor important performance metrics like engagement rates, click-through rates, conversion rates, and others. This data-driven

methodology enables ongoing sales strategy modification, guaranteeing a higher return on investment.

7. **Influencer marketing:** Social media influencers have grown to be a significant force in advertising and sales. These people can honestly market goods and services because they have a sizable and engaged fan base. Influencer marketing is a powerful tool for reaching prospective consumers because it makes use of the authority and trust influencers have established with their audience.

8. **Customer input and Product Development:** Social media gives companies a direct channel of connection with their consumers to obtain input. For the creation and enhancement of a product, this input may be quite helpful. Businesses may utilize

social media as a venue for conducting surveys-beta-testing new goods and assessing client satisfaction.

9. **Real-Time Updates and Trends:** Social media enables companies to remain flexible and react to current trends and events. Social media helps organizations to adapt and remain relevant in a continuously changing digital market, whether it's seizing a viral opportunity or quickly responding to a catastrophe.

10. **Content marketing and storytelling:** As a result of social media, conventional advertising has lost ground to content marketing and storytelling. Businesses may develop interesting stories about their goods or services to engage consumers more deeply. Platforms like LinkedIn are great for providing thought leadership

articles and industry insights, while platforms like Instagram and Pinterest are perfect for exhibiting aesthetically attractive material.

11. **Multi-Channel Sales Strategies:** The use of social media by corporations has prompted them to use such tactics. Companies may use social media networks to diversify their sales outlets rather than depending primarily on their websites or physical storefronts. This may involve utilizing Instagram to display the catalogue, Facebook Marketplace for product sales, or Twitter for sales and customer service queries.

12. **Customer advocacy:** On social media, happy customers may be effective spokespersons. Customers often post about their good interactions with brands on social media sites like Twitter and

Instagram. By encouraging consumers to use branded hashtags, contribute user-generated content, and take part in challenges and competitions, brands may take advantage of this advocacy. Customers feel a feeling of camaraderie and belonging as a result, in addition to helping to market the business.

13. **Instant Gratification and Limited-Time Offers:** Because social media is real-time, companies may use it to promote exclusive deals, flash sales, and time-limited discounts. These offers may be made to seem urgent on platforms like Twitter and Instagram Stories, enticing followers to act right away.

14. **Competitive analysis:** Social media enables companies to track and study the actions of their rivals. Companies might find areas

for development and difference by looking at the tactics used by rivals. Additionally, by scrutinizing the social media efforts of their rivals, companies may learn what strategies in their sector succeed and fail.

15. **International Market Research:** Social media is an effective technique for doing market research. Conversations may be listened to by businesses to learn about customer preferences, market trends, and new rivals. This real-time data may help organizations remain ahead of the curve by informing product development and marketing initiatives.

16. **Customer Relationship Management (CRM) System Integration:** A lot of organizations combine their social media initiatives with CRM programs. Companies may watch

consumer interactions across social media platforms and save important customer data thanks to this connectivity. CRM systems support companies in managing leads, developing connections, and customizing their sales strategies based on unique customer profiles and preferences.

17. **Localization and Personalization:** Social media enables tailored messages and specialized marketing. Companies may design location-based marketing campaigns to target certain areas or even specific individuals depending on their preferences and actions. By improving the consumer experience, personalization increases the likelihood that they will interact with the business and make a purchase.

18. **AI and chatbots:** AI-driven chatbots on social media platforms

provide round-the-clock customer service and sales help. These chatbots may respond to frequent questions, assist customers with the purchasing process, and even make product recommendations based on customer preferences. By giving customers prompt solutions to their inquiries, this automation simplifies the sales process.

As a result of its increased reach, the ability for targeted marketing, promotion of participation, and provision of useful information and insights, social media has revolutionized the sales industry. It has changed not just how companies market their goods and services, but also how consumers find, assess, and use those goods and services. Social media will probably continue to have an increasing effect on sales as technology and social platforms advance, making it a crucial part of any contemporary sales plan.

Importance of Social Selling in Today's Business Landscape

In today's commercial environment, social selling has become a vital tactic. Using social media platforms to develop connections with prospective clients, marks a fundamental change in how businesses approach sales and eventually generate income. We will look into the significance of social selling and why it has evolved into a cornerstone of contemporary sales methods in this in-depth investigation.

1. **Building Trust and Relationships:** The foundation of social selling is developing sincere bonds with clients. Social selling enables companies to engage with prospective customers on a personal level in an era when consumers are constantly exposed to marketing. A sale is often made as a result of a salesperson's ability

to participate in meaningful discussions, provide insightful commentary, and develop trusting relationships over time.

2. **Access to a Global Audience:** Social media sites have billions of individuals who are engaged in them globally. Businesses have an unmatched chance to connect with a worldwide market because of this large audience. No of the size of the business, social selling enables them to access this enormous consumer base, removing geographical restrictions that traditionally limited sales attempts.

3. **Data-Driven Insights:** Social media platforms provide a variety of analytics tools and data that enable sales professionals to make wise judgments. They may monitor consumer behaviour, measure engagement metrics, and learn more about what appeals to

their audience. With the use of this information, sales teams may concentrate on techniques that have worked well.

4. **Targeted Outreach:** Advanced targeting capabilities are available on social media networks. These attributes may be used by salespeople to locate and get in touch with people or companies who fit the profile of their ideal client. Targeting with such accuracy increases the likelihood of conversion by ensuring that outreach attempts are made to those who are more likely to be interested in the product or service being promoted.

5. **Thought leadership and content sharing:** Social marketing goes beyond blatant sales pitches. It entails disseminating useful information, including articles, instructional materials, and insights from the

business world. This elevates salespeople to the status of thought leaders in their areas. Potential clients are more inclined to believe their suggestions and take an interest in their goods or services when they see them as authorities.

6. **Real-Time Engagement:** Social media offers a real-time engagement platform. Salespeople can answer questions, deal with issues, and provide prompt support. This responsiveness encourages a pleasant customer experience and has a big impact on a prospect's choice to proceed with a transaction.

7. **Competitive edge:** Businesses that use social selling have an edge over rivals in the marketplace. Those who fall behind can lose out on chances to interact with clients who choose this contemporary strategy over conventional sales

techniques. A company may differentiate itself from rivals and present itself as a forward-thinking industry leader by being active and successful on social media.

8. **Customer-Centric Approach:** Social selling promotes a sales strategy that is focused on the needs of the customer. It moves the emphasis from promoting items to comprehending the requirements and preferences of the consumer. Salespeople may modify their language and products to line with the priorities of their prospects, resulting in a more fulfilling and customized purchasing experience.

9. **Measurable ROI:** Social selling gives a high degree of quantifiability, in contrast to conventional sales techniques. Key performance indicators (KPIs) including engagement rates,

conversion rates, and income from social selling activities may all be monitored by businesses. The social selling strategy may be continuously improved and optimized thanks to this data-driven methodology.

10. Social selling is scalable and adaptable to a range of company sizes and sectors. Whether you're a tiny business or a large organization, social selling may be customized to meet your unique requirements and goals. Additionally, it is scaleable, enabling companies to increase their social marketing efforts as they develop.

11. **Enhanced consumer knowledge:** Social selling offers a goldmine of consumer knowledge. Sales professionals may obtain a thorough awareness of the preferences, difficulties, and problems of their prospects by

closely observing social media activity. This data enables more relevant and individualized sales messages, improving conversion rates.

12. **Shortening Sales Cycles:** Conventional sales cycles can take a long time since they include many rounds of prospecting, nurturing, and closing. This process is sped up by social selling, which gives salespeople the ability to recognize warm leads more quickly and interact with them in real time. The result is a more efficient sales cycle that uses less time and money to turn leads into clients.

13. **Increasing Brand Awareness:** Social selling activity may help increase brand recognition and exposure. Sales representatives indirectly promote the company they represent when they continuously offer informative

material, interact with their audience, and position themselves as trustworthy advisers. Increased brand familiarity and even word-of-mouth recommendations may result from this.

14. **Alignment with Contemporary Purchasing Patterns:** Consumers of today are increasingly turning to the internet and social media for product research and suggestions. These contemporary purchasing habits are in line with social selling, which meets prospective consumers where they currently spend their time. Businesses are more likely to be found by prospects throughout their purchasing journey by being present and engaged on social media.

15. **Measuring ROI and Attribution:** Social selling platforms and solutions often

include powerful analytics features. This enables companies to more precisely measure the return on investment (ROI) of their social marketing activities. Sales teams may immediately link the money they earn from their social media initiatives, giving verifiable proof of the strategy's success.

16. **Scalable Lead Generation:** Social selling doesn't only include face-to-face encounters. It may also be utilized to provide a consistent flow of leads. To draw in prospective consumers, salespeople might produce and distribute lead magnets like ebooks, webinars, or whitepapers. This strategy may result in a steady stream of prospects entering the sales funnel.

17. Social selling may be used by businesses to provide effective sales training and enablement.

Organizations may make sure that their sales staff are prepared to perform in the digital environment by sharing best practices, success stories, and templates for efficient social selling.

18. **Global Networking Possibilities:** Social media eliminates geographical boundaries, enabling sales professionals to network with colleagues, subject matter experts, and possible business partners from across the globe. Through these linkages, chances for cooperation, joint ventures, and extended sales channels may arise that would not have been attainable through more conventional techniques.

In conclusion, social selling is a critical approach in today's corporate environment. It has several benefits, including improved customer insights, shortened sales cycles, increased brand recognition, and quantifiable ROI. Businesses that embrace social selling not only stay relevant as the digital world changes, but they also put themselves in a position for long-term development and success. For businesses wishing to succeed in the market of the twenty-first century, it is no longer only a choice but rather a need.

Building an Effective Social Selling Strategy

For contemporary companies wishing to succeed in the competitive digital marketplace of today, developing an effective social selling strategy is essential. Social selling is the technique of using online networks and social media platforms to locate, get in touch with, and nurture prospects to turn them into devoted consumers. Due to social media's rapid expansion, sales professionals may now use it to connect with a larger audience, forge connections, and increase sales. Take into account the following essential stages to create an efficient social selling strategy:

1. **Identify your target market:** Recognize the characteristics of your ideal client first. Find out about their characteristics, passions, problems, and motivations. This will enable you

to customize your strategy and interact on social media with the appropriate prospects.

2. **Pick the appropriate social media channels:** Do some research to find out which channels your target market uses most often. Every platform has its distinct features and user base. For instance, LinkedIn is often used for business networking, but Instagram is more popular with younger, visually inclined users. Concentrate your efforts on platforms that are compatible with the tastes of your target audience.

3. **Improve your social media profiles:** These are essentially your internet business cards. Make sure your profiles are thorough, polished, and intriguing. Use top-notch images, write a captivating bio, and provide links to pertinent articles or your website. Maintaining a solid and

coherent online presence requires consistency in branding across all channels.

4. **Disseminate useful content:** Social selling is more than simply advertising your goods or services. Deliver informative and quality material that appeals to your target audience. This might be done via blog entries, news from the sector, enlightening articles, films, or infographics. You become known as a credible expert in your field and develop credibility by continuously offering helpful material.

5. **Connect with and engage your audience:** Relationship-building and engagement are the cornerstones of social media. Engage in discussion, reply to remarks, and provide aid or direction. Utilize social listening tools to track mentions of your company name

or keywords associated with your sector of business and take the initiative to contact prospective customers. Make the communication two-way and personalize your encounters.

6. **Make use of social media advertising:** By making use of focused advertising, you may strengthen your social selling initiatives. The majority of social media sites provide effective advertising options that let you target a very particular audience based on their characteristics, interests, and behaviour. Create well-thought-out advertisements that are in line with your brand and consumer preferences to raise your exposure and produce leads.

7. **Track and assess the results of your efforts**: Regularly monitor and assess how well your social selling initiatives are doing. Engagement rates, click-through

rates, lead generation, and conversion rates are important metrics to take into account. Utilize social media analytics tools to learn what is effective and what needs to be improved. To improve your outcomes, modify your approach in light of these discoveries.

8. **Provide continuing training and support:** Because social selling is an area that is always changing, it's critical to keep your sales staff informed and provide them with the tools they need. Provide training workshops on relationship-building techniques, social media tools, and best practices. To create a culture of continual development, encourage teamwork and the sharing of success stories.

To sum up, developing a successful social selling strategy entails knowing your target market, picking the best social media sites, optimizing your profiles, sharing worthwhile content, interacting with your audience, utilizing social media advertising, tracking and evaluating your progress, and offering ongoing training and support. You may optimize your social selling efforts and promote sustainable company development by putting these measures into practice and adjusting to the ever-changing digital world.

Identifying Target Audience and Platforms

A key component of social selling is identifying target markets and distribution channels since it enables firms to interact with prospects and increase conversion rates. Understanding your target audience and choosing the best channels to reach them is crucial for a successful social selling strategy in the modern digital era. Let's take a closer look at how target audiences and platforms are identified for social selling.

1. **Market Research:** Conducting in-depth market research is the first stage in determining your target audience. This entails collecting information and insights about your sector, rivals, and future clients. You can recognize important trends, consumer preferences, and the characteristics of your target market by understanding the market landscape.

2. **Establish Buyer Personas:** Following the collection of data, it is time to develop thorough buyer personas. Based on market research, demographics, behaviour patterns, and psychographics, buyer personas are fictitious depictions of your ideal consumers. They include a range of topics, including age,

gender, location, occupation, hobbies, difficulties, inspirations, and favourite social networking sites.

3. **Examine Current Clientele:** Take a thorough look at your current clientele. Determine their common traits, purchase patterns, and the online and offline venues they commonly utilize. This study aids in the improvement of your buyer personas and offers useful insights into who your target audience may be.

4. **Social listening:** To learn more about your target audience, social listening means keeping an eye on the conversations and debates taking place on social media platforms. You may monitor keywords, brand mentions, and market trends with the use of social media listening tools, allowing you to determine the

platforms where your target audience is most engaged.

5. **Use Analytics:** Use the analytics tools made available by different social media platforms to learn more about the habits, interests, and interaction patterns of your audience. Detailed analytics dashboards are available on platforms like Facebook, Twitter, LinkedIn, and Instagram, and they give useful information on audience demographics, content reach, engagement rates, and conversion metrics.

6. **Conduct Interviews and Surveys:** By directly interacting with your target audience via interviews and surveys, you may get insightful qualitative data. These may assist in identifying certain pain spots, preferences, and insights that data alone might not be able to provide. You may modify your social selling strategy

and platform choice using the feedback you get from surveys and interviews.

7. **Competitive Analysis:** Examine the social media presence and engagement tactics of your rivals. Determine the methods and platforms they are using to connect with their intended market. With the use of this study, you may locate distinctive platforms or tactics that may not have been considered before, and you can distinguish your approach by identifying any gaps.

8. **Test and Analyze:** After you have selected a smaller number of prospective platforms based on your research into your target market, it is important to test and evaluate them. Create pertinent, compelling content and keep an eye on how it is doing across various platforms. To find out which platforms are most

successful in reaching and converting your target audience, keep an eye on important metrics like reach, engagement, conversion rates, and ROI.

9. **Modify and Improve:** The process of social selling is iterative. Maintain regular monitoring and analysis of your social selling activities, and be prepared to make changes and improvements in light of the revelations made. Customer feedback should be continuously gathered, and you should adjust your strategy to reflect the target audience's changing wants and preferences.

These procedures will help you choose the best social media sites for your social marketing activities and properly define your target market. To interact with them meaningfully and accomplish your social selling objectives, keep in mind that it's essential to comprehend your audience's preferences, behaviours, and engagement patterns.

Crafting Your Brand on Social Media

Building a solid online presence and a positive reputation requires carefully crafting your brand on social media. In the current digital era, social media platforms provide amazing chances for both people and companies to interact with their target audience, encourage participation, and improve the perception of their brand. The following are some essential stages for developing your brand on social media:

1. **Define Your Brand Identity:** It's essential to have a firm grasp of your brand's identity before launching into social media. Describe the target market, unique selling propositions, and purpose of your brand. This will assist you

in producing material that reflects your brand and appeals to the appropriate audience.

2. **Consistency is Key:** For brand growth, consistency across all social media channels is crucial. Make sure the usernames, handles, and logos you use for your profiles are the same across all platforms. Your brand identity is strengthened and brand awareness is aided by this consistency.

3. **Pick the Right Platforms:** Not every company should use every social media site. Focus your efforts on the platforms that your target demographic utilizes most. For instance, platforms like Instagram and TikTok may be preferable if you're aiming to reach a younger audience, whereas LinkedIn may be more appropriate for B2B firms.

4. **Produce Engaging Content:** Successful social media branding depends on compelling content. Create content that is specific to the platform's format and target audience. To keep your audience interested, blend textual, graphic, and video information. With useful and shareable content, try to educate, amuse, and inspire your audience.

5. **Be Authentic:** On social media, reputation and trust-building depend on authenticity. Be sincere in your communications and allow your personality to come through in your work. Avoid adopting gimmicks or a tone that is at odds with your brand's personality. Respond to feedback and communications in a timely and genuine way to engage your audience.

6. **Visual Appeal:** On social media, visuals are very important for

grabbing and holding viewers' attention. To make your material stand out, spend money on enticing photos and well-produced graphics. To develop a unified and aesthetically pleasing brand identity, keep visual branding components like colours, typefaces, and layouts constant.

7. **Establish Relationships:** Communication on social media is two-way. Spend some time interacting with your audience by addressing their queries, commenting on their posts, and engaging in dialogue. Engage in active engagement with thought leaders, brand champions, and influencers. Building sincere connections may broaden your reach and encourage brand loyalty.

8. **Monitor and Analyze:** Keep a close eye on your social media accounts to determine the success

of your branding initiatives. Track measures like interaction, reach, and conversions using analytics tools. Pay heed to criticism and change your tactics as necessary. Investigate the effects of various content formats on the overall success of your brand.

9. **Keep Current:** Social media algorithms and trends are continuously changing. Keep up with the most recent platform updates, new functions, and developing trends. To take advantage of new possibilities and make sure that your brand stays relevant and visible, adjust your strategy as necessary.

Social media brand building takes time, effort, and a deliberate strategy. You can develop a strong and identifiable brand presence, engage with your target audience, and ultimately fuel your business's success on social media by defining your brand, producing great content, being consistent, and forging connections.

Setting Measurable Goals and Key Metrics

Setting Key Metrics and Measurable Objectives for Social Selling:

Modern sales tactics now include social selling as a key component since it enables companies to interact with prospective consumers online and via social media, engage with them, and ultimately increase sales. Establishing quantifiable objectives and selecting critical indicators that may gauge the performance and impact of these initiatives are essential for ensuring the success of social selling efforts. With some examples to help you, we will discuss the significance of creating measurable objectives and important performance indicators in this reply.

Why is the importance of measurable goals in social selling?

In social selling, setting measurable objectives is essential since it gives your efforts a defined direction and makes it possible to gauge your progress and success. Your social marketing operations may lack focus without well-defined objectives, and it becomes difficult to evaluate the success of your efforts.

Setting quantifiable objectives enables you to:

1. **Establish goals:** Your social selling approach has a purpose and clarity when you have goals. They provide you with a path for achieving your goals and assist you in coordinating your efforts with more general sales objectives.

2. **Monitor progress:** Measurable objectives provide you with a point of reference so you can monitor your advancement over time. This

supports your motivation and enables you to see potential improvement or adjustment areas.

3. **Assess effectiveness:** By setting quantifiable targets, you may assess the success of your social selling initiatives. It helps you to assess if your tactics are producing the intended results and modify your strategy as necessary.

4. **Optimally distribute resources:** Setting measurable targets can help you do this. You may determine the channels, content kinds, or engagement tactics that provide the greatest results by tracking the effectiveness of various social selling initiatives. This will help you invest your time and resources in the most effective ways possible.

Choosing Important Metrics for Social Selling:

The primary metrics that will be used to gauge progress and success must be decided upon after your quantifiable objectives have been set. Your objectives and the platforms you're using will influence the metrics you use. Following are a few typical important KPIs used in social selling:

1. **Reach:** This indicator counts the total number of individuals who have seen or interacted with your social media content or brand. It helps in determining how well-known and visible your goods or services are to your intended market.

2. **Engagement:** Metrics for engagement on your social media postings include likes, comments, shares, retweets, and other interactions. These indicators show how engaged and interested your audience is with your material.

3. **Conversion Rate:** The conversion rate calculates the proportion of active users who

complete the intended activity, such as buying something, completing a form, or subscribing to a newsletter.

4. **Lead Generation:** The quantity of leads produced by social selling activity is measured using this metric. It aids in determining the efficacy of your methods for gathering prospective clients' contact information and guiding them through the sales funnel.

5. **Income**: In the end, income is an important factor in determining the return on investment of your social selling activities. By monitoring revenue, you may assess if your sales targets are being attained and determine which social selling initiatives are most profitable.

6. **Consumer Satisfaction:** Metrics that measure how successfully your social selling activities are achieving consumer

expectations include reviews, ratings, and comments. Customers who are happy with a product or service are more inclined to buy it again and to promote it publicly.

7. **Brand Awareness:** This indicator measures how well-known your brand is to your target market. Metrics like brand mentions, increases in social media followers, or website traffic from social media platforms may be used to gauge its effectiveness.

Examples of Identifying Key Metrics and Measurable Goals:

Let's say your goal for social selling is to improve the quantity of leads that are qualified and come from social media. In such an example, your quantifiable objective may be to generate 20% more leads in the next six months. Reach (to gauge the growth in the number of individuals exposed to your content), conversion rate (to gauge the proportion of engaged users who become leads), and lead generation (to track the actual number of leads created) are some key indicators for monitoring this objective.

In contrast, if your objective is to boost brand recognition via social selling, your quantifiable objective may be to see a 30% increase in brand mentions on social media platforms over three months. Reach (to gauge the increase in exposure), engagement (to gauge audience responses to your content), and brand mentions (to track the actual rise in brand mentions) are some key indicators for this objective.

In conclusion, effective social selling requires the identification of essential indicators and the setting of quantifiable targets. Your social selling activities will have a purpose and direction when you set quantifiable targets, which also make it possible to monitor and evaluate your success. You may measure the effects of your efforts and make data-driven choices to improve your social selling strategy with the aid of key indicators.

Keep in mind that you should periodically review and modify your objectives and KPIs in light of the knowledge you obtain from assessing and monitoring your social selling success.

Leveraging Social Media Channels for Sales

A key component of contemporary business and marketing is using social media networks for sales. Businesses now have a robust toolkit at their disposal to interact with their audience, increase brand recognition, and ultimately boost sales thanks to the growing popularity and reach of platforms like Facebook, Instagram, Twitter, LinkedIn, and many more. We'll examine numerous approaches, best practices, and advice for using social media to increase your sales in this thorough analysis.

1. **Know Your Audience:** Knowing your target audience intimately is essential before launching into social media. Learn about their internet habits, interests, and pain areas. Your content and engagement tactics will be guided by this information.

2. **Pick the Best Platforms:** Not all social media platforms will be appropriate for your company. Think about the platforms that are most appropriate for your product or service and where your audience is most engaged. organizations that are focused on images, for instance, would profit from Instagram, while B2B organizations might prioritize LinkedIn.

3. **Produce Top-Notch Content:** A great social media strategy is built on top-notch content. Invest in producing audience-resonating textual material, videos, and graphics. On websites like Instagram and Pinterest, visual components are very powerful.

4. Maintain a consistent brand identity across all of your social media outlets. To establish familiarity and trust with your audience, consistently use the

same logos, colour palettes, and message.

5. **Engage Your Audience:** Communication on social media is two-way. React quickly to comments, messages, and mentions. Building connections and trust with your audience may result in more purchases.

6. **Content Calendar:** To plan and schedule articles in advance, create a content calendar. By doing this, you can make sure that you maintain a regular social media presence and that your material reaches your audience when they are most engaged.

7. **Using of Hashtags:** Use hashtags to promote your work to a larger audience. Do your homework, and utilize pertinent hashtags, but don't use too many. A few thoughtful hashtags may have a greater impact than a flood of pointless ones.

8. **Paid Advertising:** Think about using the paid advertising choices that social media sites provide. These are especially useful for boosting sales since they can be finely tailored to attract certain groups.

9. **Influencer Marketing:** Work with people who are well-known in your field and have a large following. They may spread the word about your goods or services and provide significant social evidence.

10. **User-Generated material:** Inspire your clients to produce and distribute material that is relevant to your goods or services. User-generated material is genuine and has the power to sway prospective customers.

11. **Analytics and Monitoring:** To monitor the effectiveness of your postings and campaigns, use the analytics tools offered by social

media sites. To enhance your sales efforts, adapt your plan in light of the facts.

12. **A/B testing:** Try out various content genres, publishing schedules, and ad forms. By using A/B testing, you can improve your strategy and determine what appeals to your audience the most.

13. **Integration of Sales Funnel:** Align your social media strategy with your sales funnel. Utilize social media to draw in and keep the attention of prospective clients, then lead them from awareness to conversion.

14. **E-commerce Integration:** Take into account incorporating e-commerce capabilities into your social media pages if you sell things. Some systems enable users to directly purchase products by providing "shop" or "buy" buttons.

15. **Customer service:** Use social media as a medium for customer

service. Respond to questions and problems in a timely and professional manner to increase client loyalty and satisfaction.

16. **Track ROI:** It's crucial to evaluate the return on your social media marketing investments. Analyze the money earned by your social media marketing efforts, and modify your plan as necessary.

17. Keep up with the latest developments in social media. To guarantee that your initiatives continue to be successful, stay up to speed on platform upgrades, trends, and best practices.

In summary, using social media platforms to increase sales is a complex process that needs a thorough knowledge of your audience, persistent work, and the flexibility to adjust to shifting trends. Social media can be a potent tool for promoting brand awareness, traffic, and eventually revenue when used wisely.

Utilizing LinkedIn for Social Selling

Businesses and professionals wishing to forge connections, create leads, and ultimately boost sales may consider using LinkedIn for social selling. With its emphasis on business networking, LinkedIn provides a distinctive platform for social selling. We'll go into many facets of utilizing LinkedIn for social selling in this thorough review, from profile optimization to content strategies and lead-generating tactics.

1. **Improve Your LinkedIn Profile:** Your LinkedIn profile serves as your online resume. Make sure it's thorough and expert. The most important components to concentrate on are a top-notch profile photo, an arresting headline, a well-written

description, and an extensive job history.

2. **Identify Your Target Audience:** Before connecting with and interacting with others on LinkedIn, it's critical to understand who your potential clients are. Identify your target market based on their industry, job titles, size of the firm, and location.

3. **Create a Network:** Make contacts with industry experts who match the profile of your target market. Personalize your message when requesting connections to let the recipient know why you're reaching out and how it will help them.

4. **Publish valuable knowledge:** Consistently publish knowledge, ideas, and thought-provoking pieces that are relevant to your sector. This develops your

authority and maintains the interest of your network.

5. **Create and Join Groups:** LinkedIn Groups provide a forum for networking with other professionals who share your interests. Join communities for your industry and take part in conversations there.

6. Send unique messages that show your interest in the recipient and how you can provide value when contacting prospects or relationships.

7. **Interact Actively:** Interact with your network by liking and commenting on their posts. This keeps you in their minds and may result in deeper interactions.

8. **Post Long-Form Content on LinkedIn:** You may post articles there. Share in-depth analysis, case studies, and worthwhile information that showcases your knowledge.

9. **Make use of Sales Navigator:** Sales Navigator on LinkedIn is an effective resource for locating and engaging with prospects. It provides lead suggestions, connectivity with CRM, and powerful search filters.

10. **Keep an eye on Your Competitors:** Look at what your rivals are doing on LinkedIn. This might provide information about their tactics and available possibilities.

11. **Lead generation:** Locate and connect with decision-makers inside your target company using LinkedIn to generate leads.

12. **Provide Value First:** Before making your product or service pitch, give your prospects something of value. Share information, ideas, or remedies for their problems.

13. **Ask for Recommendations:** Collect endorsements and

recommendations from pleased customers or coworkers. These endorsements might strengthen your reputation.

14. **showcase Your Products/Services:** Include descriptions, photographs, and customer testimonials in the "Products" or "Services" area of your profile to showcase what you have to offer.

15. **Be Careful When Using InMail:** LinkedIn's InMail function enables you to mail others with whom you are not linked. Make sure your messages are individualized and relevant and use them rarely.

16. **Analyze and Iterate:** Review your LinkedIn efforts often and assess what is and is not working. Adapt your plan as necessary.

17. **CRM Integration:** To monitor and handle leads more efficiently, integrate LinkedIn with your

customer relationship management (CRM) system.

18. **LinkedIn Advertising:** To reach a larger audience, think about employing LinkedIn advertisements. To produce leads, you might focus on a certain industry or demography.

19. **Training and Development:** Through training courses, seminars, and programs, stay up to speed on the most recent LinkedIn features and social selling best practices.

20. Determine key performance indicators (KPIs) for your social selling initiatives, such as the quantity of leads produced, connections created, or conversions, to measure success. Monitor your progress and make strategic changes in light of the information.

In conclusion, when utilized wisely, LinkedIn is a potent medium for social selling. It's not only about connecting with as many people as you can; it's also about developing genuine connections, providing value, and making use of the platform's tools to drive leads and sales. Success in social selling on LinkedIn depends on consistency, relevance, and a customer-centric strategy.

Expanding Reach with Twitter and Instagram

A key component of any social media marketing approach should be to increase your following on Twitter and Instagram. These platforms provide distinctive capabilities and chances for companies, people, and brands to interact with a large audience. We'll examine tactics and best practices for growing your following on Twitter and Instagram in this comprehensive tutorial.

Increasing Twitter Reach:

1. **Ensure Your Profile Is Professionally Comprehensive:** Make sure your Twitter profile is comprehensive and professional, with a clear profile photo, an engaging bio, and a link to your website.

2. **Use Hashtags:** To make your material more visible to a wider audience, research relevant hashtags and use them in your tweets.

3. **Engage Regularly:** Respond to comments, retweet, and like pertinent content to interact with your audience regularly. This broadens your reach and strengthens the feeling of community.

4. **Produce High-Quality stuff:** Tweet interesting, inspiring, or educational stuff that connects with your audience. Videos and

photos with a visual component often do well.

5. **Use Twitter Lists:** Make and subscribe to Twitter lists relevant to your business or hobbies. You may be able to meet and interact with like-minded people thanks to this.

6. **Host Twitter discussions:** You may get new followers and promote your knowledge by hosting or taking part in Twitter discussions that are relevant to your field.

7. **Work with Influencers:** To get access to their fan base, and collaborate with industry influencers on shoutouts, takeovers, or co-created content.

8. **Use Twitter Ads:** Twitter gives you the choice to advertise to a wider audience. You may leverage trending topics, promoted accounts, and promoted tweets to target certain users.

9. **Track Analytics:** Use Twitter Analytics to track the effectiveness of your tweets. Adapt your plan depending on what is most effective.

Increasing Instagram Reach:

1. **Optimize Your Profile:** Include a profile image, a succinct bio, and a link to your website in your Instagram profile to make it seem visually attractive.

2. **Exceptional Visual Content:** Instagram is all visual, post movies and images of the highest quality that reflect the image of your company.

3. **Use Hashtags Carefully:** Each Instagram post is allowed up to 30 hashtags. To improve discoverability, combine hashtags from different markets.

4. **Interact with Your Audience:** Answer comments and talk to your fans. Creating a community

promotes sharing and brand loyalty.

5. **Instagram Stories and Reels:** These features provide options for fleeting and brief content. Use them to maintain audience interest and keep them informed.

6. **Work with influencers:** Instagram is a powerful platform for influencer marketing. Work together with influencers to connect with their audience and expand the impact of your business.

7. **User-Generated material:** Inspire your fans to produce material about your company or its goods. Republish user-generated material to promote authenticity and foster trust.

8. **Instagram Live:** Host Q&A sessions, product debuts, or behind-the-scenes tours with Instagram Live. This

in-the-moment interaction may draw in new followers.

9. Use Instagram Shopping to tag things in your posts and stories if you sell goods, making it simple for viewers to make purchases.

10. **Examine Insights:** Make use of Instagram Insights to see which posts do the best, when your audience is most engaged, and who your followers are.

Cross-Promotion:

1. **Connect Your Accounts:** Share links to your Twitter and Instagram profiles in your posts and profile to cross-promote your accounts.

2. **Share material Across Platforms:** Repurpose material and share it across platforms, making sure it is appropriate for the audience and format of the target medium.

3. **Promote Instagram Posts on Twitter:** To direct Twitter

followers to your Instagram content, share a tweet with a link to your Instagram post.

4. **Make Use of Integrated Tools:** To automate cross-platform publishing and interaction, make use of integrated tools and third-party applications.

In conclusion, developing your following on Twitter and Instagram calls for a calculated strategy. The secret to success is engagement and the utilization of tools like hashtags, stories, and analytics together with consistent, high-quality content. Cross-promotion between these two platforms may also assist you in reaching a larger and more varied audience. As you monitor which tactics are most effective for your particular aims and target audience, continue to adjust and improve them.

Harnessing Facebook and YouTube for Sales Success

A crucial part of many contemporary marketing methods is using Facebook and YouTube for sales accomplishment. For companies and people looking to contact, connect, and turn their target audience into consumers, these two platforms each offer unique possibilities and strategies. We'll look at tactics and best practices for using Facebook and YouTube for sales success in this complete guide.

Utilizing Facebook to Increase Sales:

1. **Establish a Business Page:** Make a polished Facebook business page for your company, complete with a distinguishable cover photo, profile photo, and contact details.

2. **Paid Advertising:** Facebook Ads are an effective strategy for contacting prospective clients

since they let you target certain demographics and interests. Think about using several ad forms, such as picture, video, and carousel advertisements.

3. **Material Strategy:** Consistently provide top-notch material that appeals to your target audience. This material may consist of product demonstrations, client endorsements, market analysis, and interesting images.

4. **Facebook Shop:** Create a Facebook Shop to display and directly sell your goods on the site. Users may have a convenient purchasing experience thanks to it.

5. **Interact with Your Audience:** Quickly reply to messages and comments. Engaging with your audience increases trust and rapport, which increases the likelihood that users will become customers.

6. **Utilize Facebook Groups:** By joining or starting groups that are relevant to your business or specialty. Participate in conversations and provide insightful commentary without explicitly endorsing your goods.

7. **Facebook Live:** Hold live events to present your items, respond to comments, and show them what your company is like behind the scenes.

8. **Use Messenger for Customer Help:** Facebook Messenger is a useful tool for offering customer help, responding to questions, and assisting prospective customers with the purchasing process.

9. **Track Analytics:** Check Facebook Insights to see how well your posts and advertising initiatives are doing. To enhance your sales efforts, adapt your plan in light of the facts.

Utilizing YouTube to Increase Sales:

1. **Establish a Professional Channel:** Create an optimized YouTube channel with a distinct banner, profile photo, and about page.

2. **High-Quality Video Content:** Since YouTube is essentially a video-sharing website, concentrates on making interesting and educational films. Showcase your goods, provide guides, and post client endorsements.

3. **Search Engine Optimization:** Improve the titles, subtitles, and tags of your videos. To help your movies rank better in search results, include relevant keywords.

4. **YouTube Advertising:** Pre-roll and display advertisements are available on YouTube. Ads may be targeted based on search history, interests, and demographics.

5. **Work with Influencers:** For product evaluations or endorsements, collaborate with YouTube influencers in your field. Their reputation and reach have a big influence on sales.

6. Engage with comments on your videos by responding to them to create a feeling of community and trust among your viewers.

7. **Playlists and Cards:** Organize your videos into playlists to make it simpler for viewers to browse your material. Use YouTube Cards to provide interactive components like links to relevant videos or your website.

8. Use YouTube Live to hold Q&A sessions, product debuts, and live product demos.

9. Examine YouTube Analytics to track the effectiveness of your videos. Recognize the kind of content that results in conversions

and adjust your approach appropriately.

Cross-Promotion:
1. **Link Your Profiles:** Share links and make mention of your other platforms in posts and videos to cross-promote your Facebook and YouTube profiles.
2. **Distribute material Between Platforms:** Repurpose material created for one platform for another, modifying it to fit the various formats and audience preferences.
3. **Use Integrated Tools:** To automate cross-platform publishing and interaction, think about using third-party tools or social media management systems.

Using Facebook and YouTube to increase sales requires a mix of paid advertising, producing original content, interacting with your audience, and making data-driven decisions. These platforms provide a wealth of chances to promote your goods or services and develop connections with your target market. You may enhance your sales efforts by using the distinct characteristics of each platform as you modify and improve your techniques.

Content Marketing and Social Selling

Two interconnected tactics, content marketing and social selling, may greatly increase your brand's online visibility, engage your audience, and increase sales. We'll go into the fundamentals and recommended methods for content marketing and social selling in this comprehensive tutorial, as well as how they work in tandem.

Content marketing includes:

1. **Content Strategy:** Content marketing starts with a clear plan of action. Determine who your target audience is, what their problems are, and what kinds of material will appeal to them.

2. **High-Quality stuff:** Produce informational, worthwhile, and relevant stuff for your audience. This may include articles, podcasts, infographics, videos, blog entries, and more.

3. Maintaining consistency is essential. Publish material often to keep readers interested and coming back for more.

4. **SEO Optimization:** To increase discoverability, optimize your content for search engines by using pertinent keywords, meta descriptions, and other SEO strategies.

5. Distribute your material via a variety of platforms, including your website, blog, social media accounts, email newsletters, and more.

6. **Narrative**: Make your material more interesting and relevant by using narrative tactics. Stories can emotionally engage your audience.

7. **Material Promotion:** To increase the reach of your material, use email marketing, social media, and even paid advertising.

8. Use enticing materials, such as ebooks, seminars, or templates, to get visitors to provide their contact details. These may be utilized to generate leads.

9. **Analytics**: Use analytics programs to gauge how well your material is doing. Analyze statistics to learn which content appeals to your audience the most.

10. **Consumer Personas:** Develop thorough consumer personas to better comprehend the requirements and preferences of your audience. Create material that speaks to these identities.

Social Selling

1. **Optimize Social accounts:** Make sure your social media accounts, particularly those on LinkedIn, are expert-looking, comprehensive, and demonstrate your competence.

2. **Identify Prospects:** Find prospective prospects via social

media sites and interact with them. Identify potential customers who suit your consumer personas.

3. **Engagement:** Participate in conversations, reply to comments, and provide information that is relevant to your target audience.

4. **Personalization:** When contacting prospects, use tailored communications that show a sincere interest in their requirements.

5. **Content sharing:** Distribute information that is helpful and relevant to your prospects. You may use original material or carefully selected stuff from other sources.

6. **Leverage Social Listening:** Use social listening tools to keep an eye on discussions relating to your field, company, or goods. You may find possible leads with this.

7. **Lead Nurturing:** Develop connections with potential

customers over time. To help clients through the purchasing process, provide them with information, advice, and support.

8. **Data and Analytics:** Use data and analytics to monitor the success of your social selling initiatives. Track key performance indicators (KPIs) like as engagement and conversion rates.

Social selling and content marketing are integrated:

1. **Instructional Content:** Content marketing may provide instructional tools that support your social selling initiatives. You may lead prospects toward blog pieces, seminars, or publications that deal with their problems.

2. **Sales Enablement:** Give your sales staff material they may use to communicate with prospects. The numerous phases of the buyer's journey should inform this content's development.

3. **Multi-Platform Promotion:** Spread the word about your material on social media to make it more visible and accessible to more people. To interact with folks who demonstrate an interest in your material, use social selling strategies.

4. Use feedback from your interactions with customers on social media to guide your content marketing approach. What queries or concerns do potential customers have? Make material that addresses these issues.

5. **Thinking Leadership:** Using content marketing, establish yourself or your company as a thinking leader in your sector. On social media, thought leaders often have an easier time interacting with and influencing prospects.

In conclusion, social selling and content marketing are complementary approaches that may result in a successful sales outcome. While social selling makes use of social media channels to find, interact with, and nurture these leads, effective content marketing develops useful resources that attract and engage prospective consumers. These techniques may boost sales and create enduring customer connections when they are combined and influenced by data and feedback.

Creating Compelling Content to Drive Sales

An essential component of promoting sales in the contemporary digital environment is the creation of appealing content. Your audience may be engaged, trusted, and eventually converted with high-quality content. We'll examine the fundamentals and top techniques for producing sales-driven content in this comprehensive guide.

1. **Know Your Audience:** Recognize your target market's characteristics, problems, and preferences. Produce material that speaks to their interests and needs.

2. **Clearly Define Your Goals:** State your content marketing objectives. Do you want to improve direct sales, provide leads, or raise brand awareness? Different content techniques are needed for different aims.

3. **Write Captivating Headlines:** The headline is what your viewers will see initially. Make catchy, succinct headlines that inspire interest or provide value.

4. **Focus on Value:** Your material should provide your readers with genuine value. Educate, amuse, or help readers with their concerns.

Rich material increases authority and trust.

5. **Storytelling:** Incorporate stories throughout your material. Stories create emotional connections and increase the relatability of your information. Share case studies, personal anecdotes, or client success stories.

6. **Use visuals:** Images, infographics, and videos may improve the attractiveness of your material and help it to communicate ideas more clearly.

7. **High-Quality Writing:** Excellent material is essential. Maintain professionalism by using good language, sentence construction, and proofreading.

8. **Consistency:** Uphold a regular publication schedule. Updated material keeps readers interested and coming back for more.

9. **SEO Optimization:** Improve your content's search engine

friendliness. To increase discoverability, use pertinent keywords, meta descriptions, and alt tags.

10. **Research and Data:** Use research and data to support your arguments. Building credibility and authority in your profession with data-driven content.

11. **Originality**: Being unique helps you stand out. Avoid plagiarism and provide original thoughts, viewpoints, and insights.

12. **User-Centric Content:** Address the demands and worries of your audience. Content that speaks directly to the difficulties and goals of your audience is more likely to convert.

13. Create engaging content types by experimenting with various content formats. Consider blog articles, videos, podcasts, ebooks, seminars, and more depending on your audience.

14. Every piece of content should have a distinct, relevant call to action (CTA). Provide instructions to your readers on the next actions they should take, such as getting a quotation, signing up for a subscription, or completing a purchase.

15. Utilize social proof by including it in your content. Potential customers may be persuaded via customer testimonials, case studies, and reviews.

16. **A/B testing:** Test and improve your material continuously. Use A/B testing to evaluate the performance of various headlines, CTA buttons, and content formats.

17. **Mobile optimization:** Make sure your material is compatible with mobile devices. A responsive design is necessary given the rising popularity of smartphones.

18. **Personalization**: Adapt your material to the tastes and actions

of certain users. Engagement and conversion rates may be greatly raised by personalized content.

19. Building trust and establishing your brand as an expert in your field is made easier by consistently delivering excellent information

20. **Measure and analyze the following:** Analytical tools may be used to monitor the effectiveness of your material. Keep track of statistics like as page visits, click-through rates, and conversion rates. Adapt your plan in light of the information.

21. **Storytelling in Sales Funnels:** Match your content to the phases of your sales funnel. Utilize narrative to lead prospects through the decision-making process, from awareness to consideration.

In conclusion, the foundation of effective sales and marketing is appealing content. You can engage your audience and advance them down the sales funnel by producing content that speaks to their requirements, uses narrative, and offers genuine value. Your content will keep generating sales and company development if you regularly measure and optimize it. Keep in mind that the most engaging content is always changing and adapting to fit the audience's shifting requirements and tastes.

Optimizing Content for Social Media Platforms

Reaching your target audience, connecting with them, and accomplishing your marketing objectives all depend on properly optimizing your content for social media platforms. Each platform has its distinctive features, target audience, and best practices. We'll examine the fundamentals and tactics for content optimization on well-known social media sites including Facebook, Twitter, Instagram, LinkedIn, and YouTube in this comprehensive tutorial.

1. Optimizing Facebook Content:

- Influential Posts:To make your material stand out in the Facebook news stream, use eye-catching images and succinct, attention-grabbing subtitles.

- Facebook gives priority to video content. On the platform, you may natively make and share videos. To interact in real-time with your audience, think about utilizing Facebook Live.

- Timing: Post at peak audience activity. You may choose the ideal moments to reach your particular audience with the aid of Facebook Insights.

- Use hashtags only when necessary. While hashtags might be useful, avoid using them excessively. To improve discoverability, include a few pertinent hashtags.
- Use Facebook Stories to provide time-sensitive updates, promotions, and ephemeral material like behind-the-scenes looks.

2. Optimizing Twitter Content:

- Short and Snappy Tweets: Create concise and interesting tweets using the character limit on Twitter. Use appropriate hashtags to get more exposure.
- Visual Materials Include pictures, GIFs, and videos in your tweets to make them more engaging.
- Engage with Trends: Add your perspective to popular discussions by adding pertinent hashtags.

- When to tweet: Timing is essential on Twitter because of its rapid speed. Use Twitter Analytics to get insights and tweet at times when your target audience is most engaged.
- Respond quickly to remarks and messages to interact with your audience.

3. Optimizing Instagram Content

- Exceptional Visuals Instagram is focused on visuals. Post high-quality images and videos that complement the style of your business.
- Maintain a consistent visual aesthetic to make your profile more aesthetically pleasing.
- Use Instagram Stories and Reels for time-sensitive material and Instagram Reels for succinct, interesting video content.
- Hashtags: To improve discoverability, research and

utilize a combination of trending and niche-specific hashtags.

- Engage with Users: Interact with your followers and reply to comments. Community development encourages brand loyalty.

4. **Optimizing the content on LinkedIn:**

- Business Tone: A professional network is LinkedIn. By emphasizing industry insights, career-related guidance, and thought leadership, your material should reflect this.

- Long Form Content You may post in-depth articles on LinkedIn's publishing platform to highlight your expertise.

- Share native video material to provide more interesting insights.

- Updates to the company page include: Update your business page often with pertinent news and information.

- LinkedIn Pulse: Contribute to LinkedIn Pulse so that your material may be seen by more people.

5. Optimizing the content on YouTube:

- High-Definition Video Production: Audio and video of high quality are essential. Spend money on quality tools and editing to produce material that looks professional.
- SEO Optimization: To increase discoverability, optimize video titles, descriptions, and tags using pertinent keywords.
- Create visually attractive thumbnails that persuade visitors to click on your videos.
- Descriptions for Videos: Write in-depth, keyword-rich video descriptions that thoroughly describe the material and promote interaction.

- Community Engagement: Participate in conversations and reply to comments to interact with your YouTube community.

6. Repurposing Cross-Platform Content

- Repurpose material and distribute it on many channels. Adjust it to the audience and format of each platform.
- Automate cross-platform publishing and interaction using third-party apps or social media management solutions.

7. Analytics and monitoring

- Use the analytics tools that each platform offers to periodically check the effectiveness of your material.
- Examine statistics to see which material is most popular with your audience and modify your approach as necessary.

In conclusion, a thorough awareness of each platform's distinctive characteristics and target audience is necessary for content optimization for social media platforms. For social media success, it is crucial to create interesting, platform-specific content and to keep abreast of each platform's changing algorithms and trends. You may produce content that successfully reaches and connects with your target audience by emphasizing audience interaction, consistency, and data-driven decision-making.

Using Influencer Marketing for Social Selling

A successful approach to social selling is influencer marketing. Utilizing influencers may increase your audience reach, foster trust, and eventually boost revenue. We'll examine the fundamentals, best practices, and tactics for using influencer marketing to support your social selling initiatives in this comprehensive book.

1. Influencer marketing: This is the practice of working with people who have a sizable and active online following on social media or other digital platforms. The authority, trustworthiness, and authenticity of these influencers in a certain niche allow them to affect the purchasing choices of their audience.

2. Finding the Correct Influencers: It's important to choose the proper influences. When identifying prospective influencers, take into account the following factors:-

- Relevance: Check to see whether the influencer's content and specialization are relevant to your goods or services.

- Audience Size: Consider if the influencer's reach corresponds to your intended market.
- Engagement: Seek influencers that have an engaged following. High engagement rates often signal a more powerful presence.
- Credibility: Check the influencer's standing and sincerity in their specialized field.
- The influencer should be compatible with the principles and personality of your business.

3. **Setting Specific Goals:** Before working with influencers, specify the goals of your influencer marketing strategy. These goals can include enhancing sales, lead generation, or brand exposure. You may assess the campaign's success using specific goals.

4. **Relationship-Building:** Use influencer marketing as an opportunity to forge new connections. Make sincere

relationships with the influencers and make sure they are fully aware of your company and items.

5. **Co-Creating Content:** Work together to co-create content that features your goods or services and is endorsed by influencers. Product reviews, guides, unboxings, and endorsements fall under this category. The material must be genuine and appealing to the influencer's audience.

6. **Trasparency**: Maintain transparency and sincerity in your relationships with influencers. Influencers should be open and honest about their connections to your company. Audiences like honesty because it fosters trust.

7. **Pay and Agreements:** Make sure influencer agreements specify pay and expectations in detail. Compensation options include cash sums, complimentary goods, and income from affiliate

programs. Make sure all conditions are negotiated beforehand.

8. Promote material developed by influencers on your social media platforms. This increases the content's impact and reach. Request that the influencer also share it with their audience.

9. **Leveraging Live Streams and Stories:** Use Facebook Live and Instagram Stories to encourage real-time interaction between influencers and their audience. Live content may increase purchases right away and is often more participatory.

10. **Affiliate marketing:** Work with influencers to establish an affiliate marketing scheme. They may offer their audience special affiliate links or codes in exchange for a cut of any purchases made via such links.

11. **Testimonials and user-generated content:** Inspire influencers to write about their first-hand interactions with your goods. Social evidence, like as reviews and user-generated material, might persuade prospective customers.

12. **Continued connection-building:** This is more important than one-time interactions with influencers. Continuous contact with their audience might result in deeper connections and a bigger sales effect.

13. **Legal Compliance:** Know the laws that apply to influencer marketing in your area. There may be several standards for openness and transparency.

Influencer marketing is a dynamic and successful approach to social selling, to sum up. It entails choosing the appropriate influencers, developing sincere connections, collaborating on interesting material, and evaluating the effectiveness of campaigns. Influencer marketing may broaden your audience, increase revenue, and improve your brand's marketability when used effectively.

Nurturing Relationships and Building Trust

Building trust and fostering connections are essential for social selling to succeed. Making genuine relationships with your audience is crucial in the age of digital commerce when face-to-face contacts are rare. In this thorough course, we'll look at the rules and tactics for social selling relationship-building and trust-building.

1. **Recognize the Value of Relationship Building:** Social selling is about establishing sincere relationships with prospective consumers rather than pushing things. The process' core component is the development of relationships.

2. **Be Aware of Your Target Audience:** Recognize the requirements, problems, and preferences of your audience. Individualize your approach for

each person to show that you care about helping them with their concerns.

3. **Personalize Your Communication:** Use names when addressing prospects and offer communications that are tailored to them. Prevent generic, universal interactions.

4. **Offer Value First:** Pay attention to providing value before marketing your goods or services. Share pertinent information, viewpoints, or solutions with prospects even before they become clients.

5. **Active Listening:** Talk less and listen more. Pay heed to the queries and worries of your potential customers. React with compassion and understanding.

6. **Regular Engagement:** Continue to interact with your network regularly. Comment on their postings, give them credit for

accomplishments, and enquire about their wellbeing.

7. Share useful material, whether it was written by you or someone else in your business. Establishing oneself as a reliable source is your aim.

8. **Be Responsive:** Answer questions and messages as soon as possible. Delays may damage trust and show disinterest.

9. **Share Success Stories:** Showcasing how your product or service has helped others, highlighting customer success stories. Social evidence is a potent strategy for establishing trust.

10. Transparency: Be open and honest about your products, costs, and rules. Trust is mostly based on sincerity.

11. **Offer Solutions:** Keep your prospects' challenges in mind at all times. Promote your good or

service as a solution rather than simply a purchase.

12. **Social listening:** Keep an eye on online forums to learn about the issues and debates in your sector. You may interact with prospects more successfully as a result.

13. **Emotional intelligence:** Recognize and relate to the feelings of your prospects. You may connect with others more deeply if you have emotional intelligence.

14. **Share Personal Stories:** Sharing personal tales humanizes your brand and makes you more relevant. It fosters a feeling of kinship.

15. **Educate and Inform:** Establish yourself as a reliable resource for knowledge and analysis in your field. Disseminate research, instructional materials, and industry trends.

16. **Consistency Across Platforms:** Keep your online persona polished and constant across all social media channels. Your brand should be consistent across your profile, message, and interactions.

17. **Deliver More Than What You Promise:** Always go above and beyond. Surpassing expectations fosters loyalty and trust.

18. **Gather and Display Testimonials:** Encourage pleased customers to provide evaluations or testimonials. Building trust by posting these recommendations on your social media platforms.

19. **Handling Objections:** Address concerns or objections respectfully and transparently. An open response to criticisms indicates your dedication to client pleasure.

20. **Social Selling Tools:** To keep track of and manage your

relationships, use social selling tools and CRM software. You can keep track of chats and follow-ups with the aid of these tools.

21. **Follow-Up:** Recall to do routine follow-up with prospects. Follow-ups regularly show that you are dedicated and interested.

22. **Leverage Video:** Make a personal connection by using video material. Prospects can see and hear you on video, which humanizes your interactions with them.

23. Create a powerful personal brand that communicates your knowledge and reliability by using personal branding. Your brand ought to reflect the principles of your business.

24. **Provide Information on hazards and Benefits:** Convey both the advantages and any possible hazards related to your

item or service. In this aspect, transparency fosters trust.

In conclusion, social selling success depends on putting the human factor first when cultivating connections and establishing trust. It's not only about making sales; it's also about building sincere relationships with your audience. You can build connections with customers that persist over time and result in more sales and brand loyalty when you constantly provide value, interact truthfully, and show empathy.

Engaging and Interacting with Prospects

One of the most important components of sales and marketing is communicating and engaging with prospects. Successful engagement promotes connections, develops trust, and results in sales. We'll examine guidelines and tactics for successfully connecting and engaging with prospects in this in-depth tutorial.

1. Recognize Your Prospects Start by carefully comprehending who your target audience is. Create thorough buyer personas that describe their needs, interests, and actions. The more familiar you are with your prospects, the more successfully you can communicate with them.

2. **Individualize Your Approach:** Address each prospect specifically in your conversations. Utilizing their name, referring to their particular requirements, or remembering their previous experiences with your company are all examples of personalization.

3. **Use a variety of channels:** Contact potential customers via email, social media, phone conversations, and in-person

meetings. Different prospects could favour various communication styles.

4. **Active Listening:** When conversing with prospects, use active listening techniques. This is listening carefully to what people have to say, following up with inquiries, and demonstrating a sincere interest in their replies.

5. **Offer Value:** The prospect should get value from every engagement. Share knowledge, ideas, or resources that meet their needs or problem areas.

6. **Ask Open-Ended inquiries:** By asking open-ended inquiries, you might encourage potential customers to talk more about their problems. Typically, these queries begin with the words "how," "what," or "why."

7. Share success stories by describing how your product or service has helped other clients. Sharing

success stories may comfort potential customers and give social evidence.

8. **Be Responsive:** Answer questions and messages as soon as possible. Communication hiccups may damage trust and show disinterest.

9. Use social listening to discover the issues that potential customers are facing and the most recent developments in your sector. This information makes it easier for you to interact.

10. **Offer Solutions:** View each conversation as a chance to address the difficulties of the prospect. Promote your good or service as the answer, not simply a purchase.

11. **Respond to concerns:** Be ready to politely and openly answer any concerns that may arise. Transparently handling

complaints may increase confidence.

12. **Emotional intelligence:** Recognize and relate to your prospects' emotions. You may establish a deeper connection with prospects by using emotional intelligence.

13. **Instructional information:** Disseminate research, instructional information, and insights from the industry. You position yourself as a subject matter authority in your profession by offering insightful information.

14. **Consistency Across Platforms:** Keep your appearance polished and consistent across all communication mediums. The ideals of your brand should be reflected in your message, branding, and interactions.

15. Use customer relationship management (CRM) software to log conversations, automate follow-ups, and categorize prospects for more individualized outreach.

16. Create a follow-up plan to ensure that prospects don't slip through the cracks. Create a methodical follow-up plan that involves ongoing contact and adding value.

17. **Engage Through Video:** By letting viewers see and hear you, video content helps to create a more personal connection with your audience. Introduce yourself, show off your products, and send follow-up communications via video.

18. **Use social selling:** Social selling entails finding and interacting with prospects on social media. Make material that will interest your audience, curate it, and take part in online debates.

19. **Leverage Automation:** Your engagement activities may be made more efficient by using automation technologies. Utilize them for lead nurturing, social media planning, and email marketing.

20. **Arrange conversations or Meetings:** Arrange phone conversations or in-person meetings as necessary. Relationships may be considerably strengthened by interpersonal encounters.

21. Use A/B testing to test various engagement strategies and messaging to see which ones connect with your prospects the most. Your approach may be improved using A/B testing.

22. **Provide Information on hazards and Benefits:** Clearly outline the advantages and possible hazards of using your

product or service. In this aspect, transparency fosters trust.

23.   **Personal Branding:** Create a powerful personal brand that showcases your professionalism and dependability. Your brand ought to reflect the principles of your business.

In conclusion, engaging and connecting with prospects is a dynamic process that emphasizes building relationships. It's about forging sincere bonds, providing value, and resolving issues. Successful engagement builds trust, which in turn may lead to successful conversions and enduring client relationships.

Establishing Credibility and Thought Leadership

In the competitive and information-driven environment of today, establishing credibility and thought leadership is essential for both people and corporations.

Credibility and thought leadership not only build audience trust but also improve your reputation by presenting you with fresh chances. We'll examine the guidelines and tactics for developing authority and thinking leadership in this comprehensive handbook.

1. **Identify Your specialty:** To begin, decide on a particular specialty or field of knowledge where you wish to build credibility. In a well defined field, being a thought leader is simpler.

2. **Deep Knowledge:** Expand your understanding of your chosen specialty. Keep up on the most recent research, trends, and market insights.

3. **Educational stuff:** Use educational stuff to impart your expertise. Blog entries, articles, whitepapers, webinars, and videos may all be included in this. The cornerstone of thought leadership is offering your audience something of value.

4. **Regular material Creation:** Create and distribute material that highlights your expertise on a regular basis. You can maintain a powerful internet presence by being consistent.

5. **Research and Data:** Provide research and data to support your material. Your views gain authority and credibility when they are supported by data.

6. Address the difficulties your audience is facing in your specialty by identifying their problems. Give answers and information that take these issues into account.

7. **Networking:** Interact with other industry experts. Join online forums, go to industry events, and create a network of like-minded people.

8. **Guest Posting:** Submit guest articles to respected websites and periodicals in your area. Your reputation is increased by offering your opinions on reputable sites.

9. **Book Authorship:** Think about penning a book on your specialty. Being a published author helps you seem more credible.

10. **Public Speaking:** Participate in webinars, seminars, and professional conferences. Speaking in front of an audience not only establishes your authority but also makes your thoughts more accessible.

11. **Social Media Presence:** Keep a polished and active profile on the social media sites that are important to your industry.

Engage your audience by sharing insightful material.

12. **Conscious Social Listening:** keep an eye on social media trends and discussions in your sector. Build relationships by taking part in conversations and contributing your ideas.

13. **Case Studies:** Provide real-world examples of your knowledge in action by sharing success stories or case studies.

14. **Be True to Yourself:** Being true to oneself is crucial. When you don't know anything, don't be afraid to confess it; nonetheless, constantly try to learn more and become better.

15. **Request Feedback:** Encourage your audience to provide suggestions and helpful criticism. It conveys that you respect their viewpoints and are willing to make improvements.

16. **Mentoring:** Provide advice or mentoring to those in your industry, especially those who are just beginning their careers. Mentoring shows your dedication to your specialty.

17. **Handle Obstacles With Grace:** Obstacles and criticism may come up. Professionally and constructively respond to them. Your credibility may be influenced by how you respond to difficulties.

18. **Sincerity and Openness:** Be sincere and open about your personal experiences and lessons learnt. Gaining your audience's trust via transparency.

19. **Continue to learn:** Keep up with the most recent advancements in your field. Thought leaders are always learning and evolving; they are not static.

20. **Invest in Continuous Improvement:** Make an investment in your professional

development by taking courses, attending seminars, and earning certifications.

21. **Accolades and Recognition:** Look for acclaim or accolades from the industry for your achievements. Awards might help you increase your authority.

22. **Partner with Other Thought Leaders:** Partnering with other thought leaders in your specialized field may increase your authority and reach.

23. **Online Presence and SEO:** Make sure that your website and social media accounts are search engine optimized. This facilitates others finding your area of expertise.

24. Measure and analyze the results of your thought leadership activities on a regular basis. Analyze audience growth, engagement analytics, and other pertinent information.

Last but not least, building credibility and thought leadership requires continuing study, content production, and networking. You can gain the trust of your audience, unlock doors to new possibilities, and establish yourself as a thought leader in your field by delivering value, solving problems, and establishing yourself as a trustworthy authority in your specialty.

Strategies for Building Trust in the Digital Era

In the digital age, trust-building is a challenging but crucial task. The quick development of technology has altered how people and organizations communicate, making trust a vital component of fruitful connections. We'll examine the methods and guidelines for fostering trust in the digital age in this extensive book.

1. **Consistency and Transparency:** It is crucial to be consistent in your activities and conversations. Create specific expectations and regularly meet them. Transparency about your goals, stances, and deeds fosters trust.

2. **Secure Data Handling:** Guard the information of your clients. Utilize secure technology, encrypt critical data, and put effective data security mechanisms into place. Trust may be severely damaged by data breaches.

3. **Privacy Policies:** Provide clear and easy access to your privacy policies. Provide consumers with opt-in and opt-out alternatives

while outlining your data collection, storage, and usage practices.

4. **Customer-Centric Approach:** Give your consumers' wants and concerns first priority. Answer their inquiries and concerns in a timely and professional manner.

5. **High-Quality material:** Offer material that is reliable, accurate, and current. Information that is misleading or false may swiftly destroy confidence.

6. **Social Proof:** To establish your credibility, use testimonies, case studies, and reviews. Trust might be influenced by other customers' favorable comments.

7. **Plain Communication:** Make sure your message is unambiguous and simple. Avoid using jargon or ambiguities that can mislead or confuse consumers.

8. **Secure Website:** To make your website secure and to guarantee

secure surfing, use SSL certificates. Online users are more likely to trust a secure website.

9. **Dependability and Consistency:** Whether it's about product quality, delivery dates, or customer service, consistently fulfill your commitments. Poor performance might undermine confidence.

10. **Develop an Online Reputation:** Make an investment in developing a good online reputation using digital platforms like forums, social media, and reviews. When receiving critical comments, act professionally.

11. **Thought Leadership:** Become recognized as a thought leader in your niche by producing quality content and market analysis.

12. **User-Friendly Website and Apps:** Make sure your online presence is intuitive, responsive, and user-friendly. Trust may be

damaged by frustrating user encounters.

13. **Customer Testimonials and Tales:** Provide actual customer testimonials and tales. Authentic stories ring true and foster trust.

14. **Secure E-commerce Transactions:** If you do e-commerce, employ secure payment gateways and make sure your clients are aware of the security protocols in place for such transactions.

15. Maintain a professional and active presence on the appropriate social media channels. Engage your audience and give them something useful.

16. Take strong cybersecurity precautions online to safeguard your digital assets and client information.

17. **Clearly Stated Return and Refund Policies:** Describe a clear and fair return and refund

policy. Respecting these rules builds confidence with online customers.

18. **Customer Assistance:** Make a variety of channels available for quick and helpful customer service. Respond quickly to questions and problems from customers.

19. **Community Engagement:** Create a network of people that support your brand. Participate in forums, social media groups, and online communities to interact with your audience. Display a sincere interest in your clients.

20. **Invest in mobile optimization:** With the use of mobile devices growing, it's important to make sure your online presence is responsive. Mobile applications and responsive web design fall under this category.

21. **Educational Content:** Produce and disseminate informational materials that answer frequent queries or issues that your audience experiences.

22. Maintain and update your website, blog, or other digital resources on a regular basis. Trust may be damaged by outdated information.

23. **Consistent Branding:** Maintain a consistent and expert image on all digital channels, including your website and social media accounts.

24. **Analyze and Adjust:** Keep tabs on the results of your trust-building initiatives. Adapt your plan in light of evidence and criticism.

In conclusion, long-term success in the digital age requires trust-building. A reliable online presence promotes client loyalty, helps you stand out in a congested digital world, and lets you take advantage of new possibilities. You may successfully traverse the challenges of the digital age and develop solid, enduring trust with your audience by following these methods and concepts.

Measurement and Analysis of Social Selling Efforts

Social selling activities must be measured and analyzed if you want to improve your techniques, figure out what's working, and get results. We'll go over the guidelines and tactics for accurately tracking and evaluating your social selling efforts in this comprehensive guide.

1. **Establish Clear and Specific goals:** Before you begin measuring, define your goals for your social selling initiatives. Do you want to improve direct sales, provide leads, or raise brand awareness? Different goals call for various measures.

2. **Determine your Key Performance Indicators (KPIs):** Select the important measurements that support your

goals. Engagement rates, lead creation, conversion rates, and income earned are typical KPIs for social selling.

3. **Use Analytics Tools:** To monitor and evaluate your efforts, make use of CRM software and social media analytics tools. For business accounts, popular networks like LinkedIn, Facebook, and Twitter include built-in statistics. Use third-party tools if you want more sophisticated information.

4. **Track Website Traffic:** Keep tabs on the volume of website traffic that is generated by your social selling initiatives. To measure this, make use of Google Analytics or other website analytics programs.

5. **Conversion Monitoring:** Implement conversion monitoring to determine how many leads or

purchases may be directly linked to your social selling efforts.

6. **Social listening:** Keep an eye on audience mood and brand mentions on social media platforms. This may provide information on how your brand is seen and if your message is being received well.

7. Use A/B testing to contrast various strategies or messaging. To determine what connects most with your audience, test variables like headlines, content kinds, and publishing timings.

8. **Sales Funnel Analysis:** Examine the effects of social selling on your sales funnel. Track prospects from their first interaction until conversion and see where they lose interest.

9. **Material Performance:** Examine indicators like likes, shares, comments, and click-through rates to see how well

your material is doing. Determine the material that generates the greatest engagement.

10. **Lead Generation:** Keep track of the quantity of leads that your social selling activities have produced. Investigate the origins and effectiveness of these leads.

11. **Customer Relationship Management (CRM) Data Analysis:** Use CRM data to analyse how social selling activities affect the sales process. Lead-to-opportunity conversion rates and sales cycle time are two examples of this.

12. **Customer Relationship Metrics:** Evaluate how well and deeply you connect with your clients. Keep track of statistics like repeat purchase rates, client retention, and satisfaction ratings.

13. **Social Media Engagement Indicators:** Evaluate engagement indicators like the rise of followers

and fans as well as likes, shares, and comments. Engagement is a sign of your audience's interest and participation.

14. **Influencer Impact:** If you collaborate with influencers, assess the results of your efforts. Monitor adjustments in leads, revenue, or engagement that are attributable to influencer relationships.

15. **Competitive Analysis:** Evaluate how well you are doing in social selling in comparison to your rivals. Examine their tactics, follower expansion, and engagement levels to spot areas that might need improvement.

16. **Sentiment Analysis:** Use sentiment analysis tools to determine whether or not your brand is being mentioned favourably or unfavourably on social media. Keep track of emotional changes over time.

17. **Modify and Improve:** Consistently evaluate the information you've obtained. Make adjustments and improve your social marketing strategy using this knowledge. Consider pivoting if particular strategies or platforms aren't producing the desired effects.

18. **Track ROI:** Determine your social selling activities' return on investment (ROI). Compare the amount of money made to the expenditures associated with social selling, such as hiring staff and paying for advertising.

19. **Summarize Your Findings and Share Your Insights by Writing Reports:** To the appropriate team members and stakeholders, distribute these reports. Building confidence inside your organization starts with reporting transparency.

20. Keep up with the most recent trends and advancements in social media and social selling with continuous learning. You can modify and improve your tactics with ongoing learning.

In conclusion, successful social selling initiatives in the digital era depend on accurate measurement and analysis. You may increase the effectiveness of your social selling activities and produce significant benefits for your company by establishing clear targets, choosing relevant KPIs, and regularly reviewing and tweaking your strategy. Since social selling is a subject that is always changing, it is essential for success to remain ahead of the curve with data-driven insights.

Optimizing Social Selling Strategies Based on Data

To guarantee that your efforts are successful and produce results, it is essential to optimize your social marketing techniques based on data. You may improve your strategy, focus on the correct prospects, and increase your return on investment by using data-driven decision-making. We'll examine the fundamentals and tactics for optimizing your social selling efforts via data analysis in this comprehensive book.

1. **Data Gathering:** Begin by gathering pertinent data. This includes interaction analytics, lead generation figures, conversion rates, information on website traffic, and any other KPIs that are consistent with your social selling goals.

2. **Establish Specific Goals:** Clearly state your social selling

goals and the key performance indicators (KPIs) that will be used to gauge your success in achieving them. Objectives can be to increase brand recognition, provide leads, or increase revenue.

3. Utilise a customer relationship management (CRM) system to gather and manage data on leads, prospects, and clients. CRM and Data Integration. For a more complete picture, combine this data with your social selling initiatives.

4. **Constant Real-Time Monitoring:** Keep an eye on all of your social selling endeavours. Track engagement and conversions in real time with analytics tools.

5. **Analytics Tools:** Make use of website analytics platforms and social media analytics tools to see how well your social selling efforts are doing. Google Analytics,

LinkedIn Analytics, and Facebook Insights are other common tools.

6. Segment your data to better understand various prospect groups. Segmentation. Based on demographics, behaviour, or amount of participation, you could segment.

7. **A/B testing:** Test out various tactics and materials. You may use A/B testing to evaluate the effectiveness of different strategies by comparing their results.

8. **Sales Funnel Analysis:** Examine the effects of your social selling efforts on each level of your sales funnel. Determine the points in the funnel where prospects stall and devise a plan to keep them going.

9. Concentrate on improving conversion rates by identifying bottlenecks and friction areas in your sales process. Apply

optimizations that are data-backed to these problems.

10. **Material Performance:** Evaluate engagement indicators like likes, shares, comments, and click-through rates to analyze how well your material is doing. Determine which of your audience's preferences for material.

11. **Lead Quality Assessment:** Determine the standard of leads produced by social selling initiatives. Find high-quality leads that are more likely to convert by using data.

12. **Customer Journey Mapping:** Draw a picture of the customer's path and note the instances at which social selling may have a significant influence. Make sure your social selling tactics follow the customer's journey.

13. **Influencer Impact:** Evaluate how influencer partnerships have

affected your social selling initiatives. Measure the impact of influencer collaborations on changes in engagement, leads, or revenue.

14. **Customer Relationship Metrics:** Analyse data to assess the quality of your interactions with customers. Examine indicators for repeat purchases, customer satisfaction ratings, and client retention rates.

15. **Social Media Engagement Indicators:** Continually evaluate social media engagement indicators, such as the increase of followers and fans, likes, shares, and comments. These measurements show how engaged and involved your audience is.

16. **Competitive Analysis:** Evaluate how well you are doing in social selling in comparison to your rivals. Examine their tactics, follower expansion, and

engagement levels to spot areas that might need improvement.

17. **Predictive Analytics:** Using previous data, use predictive analytics to forecast future results. This might assist you in making proactive choices.

18. **ROI Calculation:** To determine the return on investment (ROI) for your social selling initiatives, compare the sales income to the associated expenditures, such as staff costs and advertising expenses.

19. **Data-Driven Decision-Making:** Make decisions based on data. Based on the information you learn from data analysis, modify your plans.

20. **Reporting and Communication:** Write frequent reports that highlight the information you've learned from your data. To promote data-driven decision-making across your

organization, distribute these reports to the necessary team members and stakeholders.

21.**Ongoing Learning:** Keep up with the newest social media and social marketing trends and advancements. You can modify and improve your tactics if you keep learning.

In conclusion, data-driven social selling strategy optimization is an active, iterative process. You can optimize the effectiveness of your social selling efforts, fine-tune your strategy, and target the proper prospects by routinely gathering, analyzing, and acting on data. Effective data utilization is a critical component of social selling success in the digital era.

Overcoming Challenges in Social Selling

For salespeople and companies looking to make the most of digital platforms, overcoming social selling difficulties is crucial. Building connections online and adjusting to shifting platforms and algorithms are two particular challenges that social selling poses. We will examine the typical difficulties in social selling and solutions in this comprehensive guide.

1. **Establishing Connections in a Digital World:**
- Challenge: Since there aren't many face-to-face contacts in a virtual setting, building true connections might be difficult.
- Strategy: Emphasize empathy, customization, and active listening. Genuinely interact with potential customers. To personalize and humanize your

conversations, make use of video calls.

2. **Information Overload:**
- Problem: Online information overload makes it difficult to grab prospects' attention and make an impression.
- Strategy: Create material that is succinct and valuable. Share pertinent insights that deal with your audience's problems. Make your material unforgettable by using captivating graphics and compelling stories.

3. **Adapting to Evolving Algorithms:**
- Problem: Social media sites often modify their algorithms, which has an impact on how visible your material is.
- Strategy: Keep up with algorithm modifications and modify your approach as necessary. To adjust to algorithm adjustments, broaden

the scope of your material and interact with hot issues.

4. **Calculating ROI:**

- Difficulty: Measuring the return on investment (ROI) of social selling initiatives may be challenging.

- Strategy: Establish precise goals and KPIs, including lead generation, conversion rates, and income earned. Track and analyze these indicators often using analytics tools.

5. **Resistance to Change:**

- Problem: Sales teams and professionals may be reluctant to implement social selling strategies since they are comfortable with or at ease with more conventional techniques.

- Strategy: Help your staff realize the advantages of social marketing by providing training and education. Showcase achievements and practical examples to demonstrate the effects.

6. **Material Creation:**

- Difficulty: Producing consistently interesting and worthwhile material may be difficult and time-consuming.
- Strategy: Create a content schedule, work with content producers, and curate information that is relevant to your business. To get the most out of your material, reuse and repurpose it.

7. **Lead Generation:**

- Challenge: Using social media to generate high-quality leads needs accurate targeting and an alluring value OFFER.
- Strategy: Create buyer profiles, pinpoint your ideal demographic, and provide individualized value as your strategy. To speed up the process, use automation and lead creation technologies.

8. Harmonising Personalization and Automation:

- Challenge: It may be challenging to strike a balance between automation's efficiency and the customization required for successful social marketing.
- Strategy: Personalise initial outreach and answers to encourage real interactions, but use automation for routine chores like lead nurturing and follow-ups.

9. Privacy Issues:

- Challenge: Growing privacy issues influence social selling data collection and use.
- Strategy: Respect data privacy laws and be open when discussing data use. Provide opt-in and opt-out choices to offer your audience control.

10. **The competitive environment** is a challenge since it is difficult to stand out in the crowded social selling market.

- Strategy: Establish yourself as a thought leader in your specialized field to set yourself apart. To establish authority, provide insightful information and participate in sector conversations.

11. **Dealing with Objections:** Prospects may have reservations or scepticism regarding your goods or services. Approach objections openly and professionally. To illustrate the value of your solutions, provide statistics and case stories.

12. **Adapting to New Platforms:**

- Challenge: You must choose whether and how to include new social media platforms into your plan.

- Strategy: Keep an open mind while experimenting with different platforms. Consider their applicability to your target market and sector, and make any required adjustments.

13. **Technology Integration:**

- Difficulty: Social selling tools and CRM systems might be difficult to integrate with current procedures.
- Strategy: To guarantee a seamless transition, spend money on training and integration services. Utilise technology to its fullest extent to simplify your work.

In summary, social selling is a dynamic industry with distinct difficulties. It takes a mix of flexibility, imagination, and data-driven decision-making to overcome these obstacles. Salespeople and companies may take advantage of social selling's potential and build enduring connections with their customers by overcoming these challenges with the appropriate techniques.

Managing Time and Productivity in Social Selling

In the quick-paced world of social selling, time management and productivity are crucial. Salespeople who manage their time well may concentrate on high-value tasks, interact with prospects, and produce results. We'll examine the guidelines and tactics for social selling time and productivity management in this comprehensive guide.

1. **Establish defined goals:** The first step in any social selling campaign should be to establish clear, defined goals. Recognize your goals, whether they be boosting direct sales, generating prospects, or raising brand recognition.

2. **Create a Structured timetable:** Create a daily or weekly timetable that allows certain time blocks for

social selling chores. Having a routine in place may keep you focused and organized.

3. Determine high-value activities that directly advance your goals to prioritize them. Connecting with prospects, nurturing leads, and producing content are some examples. Put these chores ahead of lower-impact ones.

4. **Time Blocking:** Set aside particular times for various activities by using time blocking. For example, set up a block of time each for lead generation, content production, and follow-ups.

5. **Reduce Distractions:** Keep them to a minimum when working. Use website blockers if required, turn off unnecessary alerts, and establish a distraction-free workplace.

6. **Use Productivity Tools:** To simplify your job, make use of productivity software and

applications. You may keep organized by using tools like task organizers, calendars, and automation software.

7. Complete comparable chores in batches by grouping them and finishing them all at once. For instance, respond to messages and interact with prospects for a certain amount of time.

8. **Establish Time Limits:** Give each job a defined amount of time. Setting time restrictions may assist in preventing chores from growing and taking up your whole day.

9. Automate Routine chores Whenever possible, automate tedious, everyday chores. Schedules for publishing on social networking sites or automatic follow-up messages are examples of this.

10. **When It's Time to Delegate, Do It:** Delegate jobs

that don't need your attention. For instance, to free up your time, delegate administrative work to your assistant.

11. Utilise social selling technologies, such as CRM software, to automate follow-ups, monitor conversations, and expedite lead management.

12. **Establish precise Goals:** SMART goals are goals that are precise, measurable, attainable, relevant, and time-bound. Clarity and inspiration are provided by this.

13. **Learning Time:** Schedule time for ongoing education. Keep up with social selling trends and hone your abilities to adapt to the changing environment.

14. **Analyse Your Data:** Consistently examine the analytics and data generated by your social marketing initiatives. Find out

what is working and what needs to be adjusted using this information.

15. **Improve Content Creation:** Improve the way you produce content. To increase the effect of your content, create it in batches and reuse it for several channels.

16. **Network with Peers:** Interact with other people who are involved in social selling. To make use of the wisdom of the group, share your observations, advice, and difficulties.

17. **Self-Care:** Be sure to take care of yourself. Make sure you receive enough sleep, exercise, and food. For productivity, both physical and mental wellness are necessary.

18. **Use Mindfulness:** To remain focused and minimize mental clutter, use mindfulness and stress management strategies.

19. **Flexibility:** Keep an open mind about your timetable. Recognise that things won't always go

according to plan and that you may need to reevaluate your time blocks.

20. **Honour Your Successes:** Honour your successes, no matter how little they may be. Motivation and productivity may both be increased by positive reinforcement.

Finally, planning your day, maintaining organization, and concentrating on high-impact tasks are all important components of managing time and productivity in social selling. It also calls for the adaptability to change and the self-control to avoid being sidetracked. Salespeople may effectively accomplish their goals by using these tactics to maximize their social selling efforts.

Dealing with Negative Feedback and Handling Objections

The sales process, including social selling, includes dealing with negative comments and resolving objections. When handled skillfully, negative comments and objections provide possibilities for improvement and may result in more successful conversions. This comprehensive article will go over the ideas and tactics for addressing objections and bad reviews in social selling.

Dealing with Unfavourable Reaction:

1. **Remain Professional and Calm When Receiving Negative Comments:** Remain professional and calm. Avert emotional reactions since they might make the issue worse.

2. **Actively Listen:** Take the time to comprehend the comments or critiques. If clarification is required, ask clarifying questions and demonstrate your genuine interest in the client's problems.

3. **Express Regret and Acknowledgment:** If the criticism relates to a real issue or problem, express regret and acknowledgment. This indicates your dedication to finding solutions.

4. **Provide remedies:** Make suggestions for workable remedies to the issues or worries expressed in the comments. Demonstrate your initiative in problem-solving.

5. **Use Feedback for Improvement:** Consider constructive criticism as a chance to become better. Make use of it to improve your goods, services, or operations.

6. **Address openly, fix Privately:** If the unfavorable review was made on social media in a public forum, recognize it openly and make an offer to continue the discussion via email or private messaging to fix the situation.

7. **Encourage Additional Communication:** Encourage the client to get in touch with you personally to go over their issues in greater depth. This enables you to provide more customized assistance.

Taking Care of Objections:

1. **Expect and Get Ready:** Recognise typical objections that might come up throughout the sales process. Prepare your answers and solutions beforehand.

2. **Active Listening:** When a potential customer objects, pay close attention to what they have

to say. To find the root causes, use open-ended inquiries.

3. **Empathise**: Express understanding and empathy. Recognize the buyer's worries and present oneself as their buddy in locating the ideal answer.

4. **Respond to objections Transparency:** When responding to criticism, be truthful and open. To allay fears, provide information that is accurate and understandable.

5. **Emphasise Benefits:** Stress the advantages and worth of your item or service. Describe how it may help the prospect with their unique wants or pain spots.

6. Share success stories and case studies that illustrate how others have overcome comparable resistance and obtained desirable results.

7. **Request Clarification:** If the complaint is ambiguous or

unclear, request clarification from the potential customer to better comprehend their worries.

8. Apply the "Feel-Felt-Found" technique: to relate to the prospect by mentioning similar experiences that others have had, describing those experiences, and describing the results of adopting your product or service.

9. **Trial Period or Proof:** To demonstrate how your service allays its worries, give a trial period or supply proof, such as a demo or sample.

10. **Create a Sense of Urgency:** Procrastination is often a factor in objections. Instill a feeling of urgency by emphasizing the advantages of taking quick action.

11. **Deal with Objections in Stages:** If the prospect has many objections, deal with each one separately. Getting over one

skepticism might make handling the rest simpler.

12.**Accept the Prospect's choice:** Ultimately, regardless of whether the prospect decides to proceed or not, accept their choice. Keep the possibility of further interaction open.

13.**Constant Coaching:** Constantly teach and educate your sales staff on how to handle objections. To improve abilities, practice objection situations.

In conclusion, managing objections and coping with unfavorable criticism are crucial social selling abilities. Utilize the possibility for progress presented by feedback by approaching it with a professional and sympathetic perspective. When resolving objections, pay close attention, show empathy, and address issues openly while concentrating on the benefits that your product or service may provide. You may transform objections into opportunities and improve client connections by using these techniques.

Scaling Social Selling for Long-Term Success

Extending your efforts, streamlining procedures, and cultivating connections over time are all important components of scaling social selling for long-term success.

Social selling is a sustainable method for creating long-lasting relationships and generating cash rather than simply a quick fix. We'll examine the fundamentals and tactics for growing social selling for long-term success in this comprehensive book.

1. **Establish Stated Goals:** State your long-term goals for social selling in a clearly defined manner. Do you want to improve direct sales, provide leads, or raise

brand awareness? Your strategy is guided by your goals.

2. **Create a Stable Foundation:** Before scaling, make sure your foundation is stable. Define your target market, create a credible web presence, and decide on your essential messages.

3. **Create Content Plan:** Create a content plan that supports your long-term objectives. Create a regular flow of informative, interesting, and relevant information for your audience.

4. **Scalable Procedures:** Design workflows and procedures that can expand as your social selling initiatives do. Activities like lead generation, content production, and engagement should be supported by these procedures.

5. **Leverage Technology:** To automate processes and save time, make use of social selling tools, CRM programs, and automation.

These solutions can support lead management, interaction tracking, and follow-up automation.

6. **Data-Driven Approach:** Adopt data analysis to continuously improve your plan. Measure KPIs often, monitor engagement, and modify your strategy in light of new information.

7. **Scalable Team:** Make sure your team is scalable if you have one. As your social selling efforts grow, prepare your team members by training them and providing them with the necessary tools.

8. **Consistent Branding:** Keep your branding consistent across all digital channels to project a cohesive and expert picture.

9. **Work in Partnership with Other Teams:** Partner with the marketing, customer service, and other pertinent teams. Your social marketing activities may be more

effective if cross-functional cooperation is used.

10. **Develop thinking Leadership:** Position your business or yourself as a thinking leader in your specialized field. Long-term credibility is developed by sharing insightful knowledge and domain authority.

11. **Focus on Relationship Building:** Make an effort to establish and maintain connections with your audience. Over time, consistent participation creates loyalty and trust.

12. **Consider Extending Across Platforms:** As your skills and resources increase, think about extending your social selling efforts to new platforms or channels that are relevant to your target market.

13. **Track Industry Trends:** Keep up with changes in the social selling environment and industry

trends. Adjust your tactics to take advantage of new chances.

14. **A/B Testing:** Continue A/B testing experiments to hone your strategy. To find out what resonates the most, experiment with multiple content kinds, publishing times, and messages.

15. **Customer Feedback Loop:** Establish an ongoing dialogue with your clients. Encourage comments, pay attention to their viewpoints, and make use of their ideas to improve your services.

16. **Maintain Transparency:** Long-term success depends on your interactions being transparent. Be honest about your aims, services, and goods.

17. **Long-Term Content Planning:** Create an overall strategy for your content. Think about how your material may change over time while still being relevant to your audience.

18. **Continuous Learning:** Keep up with the most recent social marketing trends and advancements. Your ability to adapt to change and stay competitive is ensured by continuous learning.

19. **Track and Measure ROI:** Monitor the ROI of your social selling initiatives continuously. Analyze their impact on revenue and overall corporate goals.

20. **Regularly Update Your Approach:** As demands change, your social selling approach should adapt. Update your strategy often in light of new information and criticism.

In conclusion, strategic planning, technology use, and relationship-building are all necessary for growing social selling to achieve long-term success. It's not only about securing quick benefits; it's also about fostering and growing your online presence over time. You can develop a scalable social selling platform that generates results and forges enduring relationships with your audience by using these tactics.

Conclusion

The book ***"Social Selling in the Digital Era: Using Social Media to Drive Sales and Grow Your Business"*** has explored social media's revolutionary potential in the areas of sales and company expansion in great detail. The book has taken us on a tour through the dynamic world of social selling, demonstrating the methods, techniques, and ideas that are the foundation of achievement in the modern world.

We've learned from the pages of this book that social selling is not just a fad but a fundamental change in how companies and salespeople interact with their customers. We have investigated a wide range of social media sites, including ***LinkedIn, Twitter, Facebook, Instagram, and YouTube,*** to better understand their potential and the best ways to use them.

As essential elements of successful social selling, the significance of content marketing thought leadership, and engagement methods has been emphasised. We've looked at the nuances of creating engaging material, optimizing it for different platforms, and creating a strong online presence. Through this process, developing credibility, fostering relationships, and trust have been key elements.

Demystifying social selling measurement and analysis helps readers make data-driven choices and iteratively improve their tactics. We have uncovered the intricacies of time management and productivity, highlighting the value of planning, technology, and adaptability in this quickly changing environment.

It has been suggested that handling objections and responding to unfavorable criticism are chances for development, wherein empathy, openness, and good communication may transform objections into fruitful talks. The need to scale social selling for long-term success has also been emphasized in the book, along with the relevance of establishing precise goals, developing scaleable procedures, using technology, and cultivating connections over time.

As we come to a close on this trip, it's critical to understand that social selling is a dynamic activity. It's a dynamic field that needs ongoing learning and adjustment. Rapid change characterizes the digital world, and keeping up with the times necessitates a dedication to continual learning.

Social selling is now essential to the success of organizations and salespeople in the digital era when technology links us to one another and the internet's power is at our fingertips. This book has given you the skills and information necessary to succeed in this dynamic environment where authenticity, value, and connections rule supreme.

"Social Selling in the Digital Era" provides you with the insights, tactics, and concepts required to succeed in the world of social selling, whether you're an experienced sales professional wanting to adapt to the digital era or an entrepreneur hoping to build your firm. It's more than simply a book; it's a road plan for achievement in the dynamic and always-changing world of digital sales and company expansion.

As you begin your *social selling journey,* keep in mind that establishing trust, providing value, and being flexible is essential for long-term success. As you travel the thrilling landscape of social selling in the digital age, let this book be your map, your inspiration, and your constant companion. Accept the power of social media, and use it to boost your company's expansion and sales. Your adventure has only just started, and there are many options in the digital age. Good luck with your social selling endeavor!